Native Americans on United States Coinage
Second Edition

Victor E. Sower, Ph.D., C.Q.E.

ISBN: 978-1-72926-679-3

DEDICATION

This book is dedicated to my Native American son-in-law, Carey Fuller, and my three Native American grandchildren, Elizabeth, Joshua, and Elijah Fuller.

CONTENTS

ACKNOWLEDGMENTS

I acknowledge and appreciate the support of my wife, Judy, who has always supported me in all of my endeavors. Without that support this book would never have been written. Her comments on the many versions of the manuscript were very helpful.

I also acknowledge and thank Dr. Frank K. Fair, Ph.D., Distinguished Professor Emeritus of Philosophy at Sam Houston State University who reviewed an early manuscript of this book. His insightful comments and suggestions were important to the quality of this book.

Victor E. Sower

INTRODUCTION

This book documents the depiction of Native Americans on United States coins. Some depictions are of actual Native American individuals, others represent a composite of known Native American individuals, while some are idealized or generalized images.

Some of the coins are regular issues of the United States Mint intended primarily for circulation. These coins are usually included in uncirculated and proof editions by the Mint. Other coins are commemoratives or collectables which are issued only in uncirculated and/or mint editions. While these are also legal tender, their collection value exceeds their denominated value, and in some cases the "melt value" of the metal from which they were coined.

We begin with the Regular Issues which depict actual Native American subjects. This section is followed by Regular Issues which depict idealized images of Native Americans. The next group, referred to as "imposters" represent depictions that appear to be Native American, but really are images of Liberty with an added feather headdress.

The next section covers the commemorative half dollars followed by a section on the two collectable silver dollars depicting Native Americans. The final section covers the issues through 2018 in the Native American $1 Coin Program. These coins share a common obverse design depicting Sacagawea and her child but with a different reverse design each year.

REGULAR ISSUES

Since 1859, six standard issue coins have been produced by the United States mint that are characterized as depicting Native Americans. The Indian Head cent (1859-1909), the gold eagle (1907-1933), the quarter eagle (1908-1929), the half eagle (1908-1929), the Indian Head or Buffalo nickel (1913-1938), and the relatively recently issued Sacagawea dollar (2000). The quarter and half eagles share the same obverse design. But two of the six are "imposters" and do not represent Native Americans at all. Two others represent idealized depictions of Native Americans. The remaining two can claim to be real depictions of Native Americans. Which are which?

The Real Depictions

The Indian Head or Buffalo Nickel

The celebrated sculptor, James Earle Fraser was the designer of the Indian Head or Buffalo nickel. He used three different Native American chiefs as models for the obverse design: Iron Tail, Two Moons, and another not named by the designer but thought to be Big Tree.

Iron Tail (Sinte Maza), born around 1842, was an Oglala Lakota. He was characterized as being a wise counselor and diplomat. He gained widespread fame when he became part of Buffalo Bill Cody's Wild West Show which traveled the world. Big Tree was a Kiowa; and Two Moons, a Cheyenne.

The model for the bison or buffalo on the reverse of the coin was Black Diamond, a resident of the New York Zoological Gardens. The coin is composed of 0.750 copper and 0.250 nickel. It weighs 5 grams and is 21.2 mm in diameter. The coin was introduced in 1913 with the buffalo standing on a mound (variety I). Later in the same year, the design was changed to show the buffalo standing on a smaller mound with a thin straight line as its base. The Buffalo nickel was produced until 1938 when it was replaced by the Jefferson nickel.

The Sacagawea Dollar

In 2000, the United States Mint released the Sacagawea Golden Dollar, which featured a portrait of Sacagawea carrying her infant son, Jean-Baptiste, on the obverse and an eagle on the reverse. The coin was authorized under The United States $1 Coin Act of 1997, Section 4 of the 50 States Commerative Coin Program Act.

Sacagawea was a member of the Shoshone tribe. She served as a guide and an interpreter for the Lewis and Clark Expedition from 1804 to 1806. The design of the Sacagawea dollar coin was the result of a competition held by the United States Mint. The obverse design winner was Glenna Goodacre. She used Randy'L Hedow Teton, a Shoshone woman attending the University of New Mexico, as her model. Thomas D. Rogers, Sr. is the designer of the reverse of the coin.

The coin is a clad design with a solid copper core clad with an alloy of 0.770 copper, 0.040 nickel, 0.070 manganese, and 0.120 zinc. It weighs 8.1 grams and is 26.5 mm in diameter. The golden color of the coin was mandated by Congress in the United States Dollar Coin Act of 1997.

The Idealized Depictions

The Indian Head Quarter and Half Eagle

The Indian Head quarter ($2.50) and half ($5.00) eagle gold coins were designed by sculptor Bela Lyon Pratt of Boston. The idea for the unique incuse design came from Dr. William Sturgis Bigelow. This novel design led to the demise of the series because of complaints that the coins did not stack well and that contaminants could lodge in the recessed design thereby spreading disease. Both coins were introduced in 1908 and were produced until 1929. *The New York Times* in 1908 characterized the obverse design as "a characteristic head of an Indian Chief, with headdress of feathers and prominent masculine features" – an idealized design. The quarter eagle coin is composed of 0.900 gold and 0.100 copper. It weighs 4.18 grams (0.12094 oz. of pure gold) and is 18 mm in diameter. The half eagle coin is also 0.900 gold and 0.100 copper. It weighs 8.359 grams (0.24187 oz. of pure gold) and is 21.6 mm in diameter.

The Imposters

The Indian Head Cent

The Indian Head small cent was designed by James B. Longacre. It was introduced in 1859 in a copper-nickel alloy with a laurel wreath on the reverse. In 1860 the reverse design was modified to include a shield at the top of an oak wreath. In 1864, the metal of the coin was changed to a bronze alloy. Both the copper-nickel and bronze versions were produced in 1864. While the coin is called an Indian Head cent, in actuality the portrait on the obverse is of Liberty wearing an Indian headdress.

The copper-nickel cent is composed of 0.880 copper and 0.120 nickel. It weighs 4.67 grams and is 19 mm in diameter. The bronze cent is composed of 0.950 copper and 0.050 tin. It weighs 3.11 grams and is 19 mm in diameter.

The Indian Head Gold Eagle

The Indian Head gold eagle was designed by one of America's greatest sculptures, Augustus Saint-Gaudens. Saint-Gaudens was given the commission by President Theodore Roosevelt who wanted to transform America's coinage to imitate ancient Greek coins. The obverse design is not a portrait of a Native American but of Liberty in an Indian headdress.

Because Roosevelt objected to the use of God's name on coinage, "In God We Trust" was omitted from this coin until 1908 when Congress passed a bill restoring the motto. The coin is composed of 0.900 gold and 0.100 copper. It weighs 16.718 grams (0.48375 oz. of pure gold) and is 27 mm in diameter.

COMMERATIVE HALF DOLLAR ISSUES

In addition to the "regular issue' coins discussed previously, there have been a number of commemorative coins issued which depict Native Americans. All of the half-dollar coins were struck in 0.9000 fine silver weighing 12.5 grams.

Arkansas Centennial Half Dollar

The Arkansas Centennial Half Dollar was struck from 1935 through 1939 to commemorate the 100th anniversary of Arkansas' entry into the Union. The obverse contains a double profile of two figures: Lady Liberty representing 1936 and a Quapaw Indian representing 1836. The reverse is contains a large eagle in front of a rising sun with the name Arkansas above. Both the obverse and reverse designs are by Edward Everett Burr and Emily Bates.

Daniel Boone Bicentennial Half Dollar

The Daniel Boone Bicentennial Half Dollar was struck from 1934 through 1938 in honor of the famous American pioneer Daniel Boone. The obverse of the coin depicts a bust of Daniel Boone. The reverse design consists of an image of Daniel Boone holding a chart of Kentucky and a musket facing Chief Black Fish, war chief of the Chillicothe division of the Shawnee tribe. Both the obverse and reverse were designed by Augustus Lukemann. The inscriptions read "In God We Trust", "E Pluribus Unum", "Daniel Boone Bicentennial Pioneer Year", and the date of issue.

Long Island Tercentenary Half Dollar

The Long Island Tercentenary Half Dollar was issued in 1936 to celebrate the 300th anniversary of the European American settlement of Long Island, NY. The obverse depicts a Dutch colonist and an Algonquin tribesman. The reverse depicts a Dutch sailing ship. Both the obverse and reverse were designed by Howard Kenneth Weinman.

Missouri Centennial Half Dollar

The Missouri Centennial Half Dollar was issued in 1921 to celebrate the 100th anniversary of Missouri's entry into the Union. The obverse depicts frontiersman Daniel Boone wearing his trademark coonskin cap. The reverse depicts Daniel Boone bearing a rifle and pointing westward and an American Indian bearing a shield and a peace pipe. Both the obverse and reverse were designed by Robert Aitken.

Oregon Trail Memorial Half Dollar

The Oregon Trail Memorial Half Dollar was intermittently issued by the U.S. Mint from 1926 through 1939 to commemorate the pioneers who traveled west along the 2,000-mile trail. Opinion is divided as to which side is the obverse and which side is the reverse. This has led to using "wagon side" and "Indian side." The wagon side depicts an ox-drawn Conestoga wagon heading west into the setting sun. The Indian side depicts a Native American man in feathered headdress with bow in hand standing proudly before a borderless map of the continental United States. Both the obverse and reverse were designed by James Earle Fraser, who also designed the Indian Head (Buffalo) Nickel, and Laura Gardin Fraser.

Providence Rhode Island Tercentenary Half Dollar

The Providence Rhode Island Tercentenary half dollar was issued in 1936 to commemorate the 300th anniversary of the founding of the New England city by Roger Williams. The obverse depicts Roger Williams landing in the New World with *Bible* in hand and being greeted by a Native American with a welcoming extended hand. The reverse depicts the state seal of Rhode Island. The coin was designed by John Howard Benson and Arthur Graham Carey.

COLLECTABLE SILVER DOLLAR ISSUE

Collectable silver dollars are issued by the U.S. Mint in uncirculated and proof editions. While they are legal tender, none were struck for regular issue. All of the collectable silver dollars contain 26.7300 grams of 0.9000 fine silver. Two fairly recent collectable silver dollars depict Native Americans.

Buffalo (Indian Head) Silver Dollar

The 2001 Buffalo (Indian Head) collectable silver dollar is an adaptation of the design by James Earle Fraser for the Buffalo (Indian Head) Nickel issued from 1913-1938. See the entry for Indian Head (Buffalo) Nickel for design information. The law authorizing the minting of this coin specified that the funds raised from sales were to be used by the National Museum of the American Indian in Washington, DC to support its ongoing educational activities.

Jamestown 400th Anniversary Silver Dollar

The 2007 Jamestown 400th Anniversary Silver Dollar commemorates the founding of the first permanent English colony in the New World at Jamestown, Virginia. This obverse design depicts Jamestown with three individuals, a European settler, an African-

American laborer, and a Native American, who were instrumental in building this country.

The obverse was designed by Donna Weaver and sculpted and engraved by Don Everhart. The reverse was designed by Susan Gamble and sculpted by Charles L. Vickers. Funds from the sale of the coin benefit the Jamestown-Yorktown Foundation of the Commonwealth of Virginia, the Secretary of the Interior and the Association for Preservation of Virginia Antiquities.

THE NATIVE AMERICAN $1 COIN PROGRAM

The Native American $1 Coin Program is a variation on the Sacagawea dollar. All of the coins in this series have a common obverse design.

Authorized by Public Law 110-82, the Native American $1 Coin Program celebrates the important contributions made by Native American tribes and individual Native Americans to the history and development of the United States. The public law mandates that a reverse design, with an image emblematic of one important Native American or Native American contribution to the history and development of the United States, be issued at a rate of once a year. The series began with the 2009 issue.

The obverse (heads) design of all the Native American $1 Coin continues to feature the central figure "Sacagawea" carrying her infant son, Jean Baptiste. Inscriptions are "LIBERTY" and "IN GOD WE TRUST," while the year, mint mark, and "E PLURIBUS UNUM" are incused on the coin's edge.

Through 2018, 10 coins have been issued. The United States Mint has not yet said how many different coins will comprise the complete set.

2009 Three Sisters Agriculture

The reverse design features a Native American woman planting seeds in a field of corn, beans, and squash. The reverse was designed by Norman Nemeth.

"Maize was domesticated in central Mexico and spread from the southwest through

North America, along with symbiotic "Three Sisters" agriculture, in which corn, beans and squash growing in the same mound enhanced the productivity of each plant. Native American skill in agriculture provided the margin of survival for the early European colonists, either through trade or direct sharing of expertise, and agricultural products native to the Americas quickly became staples throughout Europe.

Three Sisters symbiotic agriculture—planting corn, climbing beans and squash together in the same plot—also originated in central Mexico and probably spread simultaneously with the corn. In this efficient planting method, corn stalks provided support for the bean vines, which added nitrogen to the soil. Squash provided ground cover, which discouraged weeds. Productivity was much higher (by some estimates as much as 30 percent) for the three grown together than each grown separately.

Agriculture has always been an important subject in Native American culture. Native American culture emphasizes living with the land and understanding the surrounding natural resources. When Europeans first arrived in the "New World," one of the largest contributions and benefits of their relationships with Native Americans was the sharing of agricultural information. It is widely acknowledged that colonists would not have survived in the New World without the support and knowledge gained from Native American agricultural techniques.

Native Americans practiced crop rotation, round cropping, hybridizations, seed development, irrigation methods, and many other agricultural techniques that are still used today."[1]

---

[1] https://www.usmint.gov/coins/coin-medal-programs/native-american-dollar-coins/2009-three-sisters-agriculture

2010 Great Law of Peace

The reverse design features an image of the Hiawatha Belt with 5 arrows bound together. The reverse was designed by Thomas Cleveland and sculpted by Charles L. Vickers.

"The Haudenosaunee Confederation, also known as the Iroquois Confederacy of upstate New York, was remarkable for being founded by 2 historic figures, the Peacemaker and his Onondaga spokesman, Hiawatha, who spent years preaching the need for a league. The Peacemaker sealed the treaty by symbolically burying weapons at the foot of a Great White Pine, or Great Tree of Peace, whose 5-needle clusters stood for the original 5 nations: Mohawk, Oneida, Onondaga, Cayuga and Seneca.

The Hiawatha Belt is a visual record of the creation of the Haudenosaunee dating back to the early 1400s, with 5 symbols representing the 5 original Nations. The Haudenosaunee symbol, the Great White Pine, is the central figure on the belt, also representing the Onondaga Nation. The four square symbols on the belt represent the Mohawk, Oneida, Cayuga and Seneca nations. The bundle of 5 arrows symbolizes strength in unity for the Iroquois Confederacy.

Northern European settlers from France, England and the Netherlands interacted with the Haudenosaunee as a separate diplomatic power. The success of the confederation showed the colonists that the Greek confederacies they had read about in the histories of Polybius were a viable political alternative to monarchy. The symbolism of the Great Tree of Peace and eagle sitting on its top were adopted as national icons during the American Revolution.

Some early narratives by explorers and missionaries introduced Europe to Native American societies which practiced equality and democratic self-government. These narratives quickly found their way into classics of European thought, including Sir Thomas More's 'Utopia' and Montaigne's 'Essays.' John Locke cited the Huron election of its chiefs in his refutation of the Divine Right of Kings.

When the newly independent Americans devised a continental government, they may have seen in these native societies living examples of the successful confederacies that they admired in the ancient Greek histories. Many tribal groups established confederations often based on linguistic affinity. One of the most famous and powerful of these Native leagues was the Iroquois Confederacy, known to its members as the Haudenosaunee (People of the Longhouse) or the Six Nations."[2]

2011 Wampanoag Treaty of 1621

The reverse design features hands of the Supreme Sachem Ousamequin Massasoit and Governor John Carver, symbolically offering the ceremonial peace pipe after the initiation of the first formal written peace alliance between the Wampanoag tribe and the European settlers. The reverse was designed by Richard Masters and sculpted and engraved by Joseph Menna.

"Within Native American culture, the ability to make peace was historically as highly prized as leadership in war and often conducted by a separate peace chief, who stepped in when the time for the warriors had passed. For centuries, tribes created alliances with each other that spanned hundreds of miles. One of the first treaties for a mutual alliance with settlers in what became the United States of America occurred between the Puritan settlers at Plymouth and the Massasoit of the Pokanoket Wampanoag in 1621. Historians credit

---

[2] https://www.usmint.gov/coins/coin-medal-programs/native-american-dollar-coins/2010-great-tree-of-peace

the alliance with the Massasoit with ensuring survival of the Plymouth colony.

From the Declaration of Independence until 1868, the U.S. made some 370 treaties with Indian tribes. Congress suspended formal treaty-making in 1868, but since then, government-to-government relations between the U.S. and sovereign tribes have taken a variety of other legal forms. Current U.S. policy states that federal relations with recognized tribes are conducted on a government-to-government basis.

In the spring of 1621, Ousamequin, the Massasoit (a title meaning head chief) of the Wampanoag Indians, made a formal treaty with the English who settled at Patuxet (in what is now Plymouth, Massachusetts). The document might well be the first written treaty between an indigenous people and European settlers in what is now the U.S. It consisted of six provisions, recorded in William Bradford's "History of Plimoth Plantation."

Massasoit promised to defend the Plymouth settlers against hostile tribes in return for their intervention if his people were attacked. His intermediaries—Tisquantum, Samoset and Hobbamack—gave the settlers invaluable tips on survival.

The Plymouth settlers honored the treaty later that summer by coming to Massasoit's rescue when they thought he had been captured by enemies. In mid-October 1621, Massasoit and 90 of his tribesmen celebrated a harvest feast at Plymouth for three days (a traditional English folk celebration). The 1621 feast inspired the legend of the first Thanksgiving, as it was called 220 years later. The treaty at Patuxet lasted more than 50 years."[3]

---

[3] https://www.usmint.gov/coins/coin-medal-programs/native-american-dollar-coins/2011-wampanoag-nation-alliance-with-plymouth-bay

2012 Trade Routes in the 17th Century

The reverse design features a Native American and horse in profile with horses running in the background, representing the historical spread of the horse. The reverse was designed by Thomas Cleveland and sculpted and engraved by Phebe Hemphill.

"American Indians maintained widespread trans-continental, inter-tribal trade for more than a millennium. The Native American trade infrastructure became the channel by which exploration, settlement and economic development in the colonial period — and later of the young republic — ultimately thrived. When early European traders ventured from eastern city centers into the interior lands, they followed trading routes still in use, often in the company of Native American guides and traders who had used them for generations. In addition, they encountered an ecosystem and Native American culture already being transformed by European goods that had moved along these trading routes long before Europeans themselves arrived in the interior regions.

These routes showed the way to European explorers and traders and marked the corridors for future east-west travel. The Lewis and Clark Expedition in 1803 followed parts of this trail. This cross-continental trade infrastructure culminated in the construction of the modern-day interstate highway system. Trading routes centered on Zuni Pueblo in the Four Corners region of the southwest and the Mojave bead route to the California coast were incorporated into the Old Spanish Trail (now a National Park Service historic trail). The Old Snake Trade Route connected the pueblos of New Mexico north to the Mandan villages in the present-day Dakotas, branching to the west in present-day Wyoming and reaching the Columbia River at The Dalles in Oregon.

Of all the goods traded throughout the continent, the horse, spread by Indian tribes through Native American trade routes, is perhaps the most significant. Thanks to inter-tribal trade, horses had crossed the Rio Grande by 1600. This trade received a massive infusion in 1680, when the Pueblo Revolt released thousands of horses from the mission herds into Native American hands.

The horse became perhaps the most sought-after commodity in inter-tribal trade. The horse's spread in Native American hands was so prodigious that it became the primary means of transportation and the nucleus of the ranching economy already underway in the western territories. In the south, the Caddo trade center became a major entry point for the horse. Trade up the Old Snake Route brought horses as far north as the Mandan in North Dakota, who supplied them to the Lakota and Blackfeet. A parallel inter-mountain route brought horses to the northwest. By the time Lewis and Clark wintered with the Mandan in 1803, they encountered a well-established horse culture. These long-established Native American trade routes also provided the path for this primary means of transportation — a significant contribution to opening up the continental interior to the developing Nation."[4]

2013 1778 Treaty with the Delawares

The reverse design features a turkey, howling wolf and turtle (all symbols of the clans of the Delaware Tribe), and a ring of 13 stars to represent the Colonies. The reverse was designed by Susan Gamble and sculpted and engraved by Phepe Hemphill.

"When the American Revolution established a new sovereign government on the North American continent, its founders acknowledged the significance of Indian tribes as the new

---

[4] https://www.usmint.gov/coins/coin-medal-programs/native-american-dollar-coins/2012-trade-routes-17th-century

United States of America dealt with tribes government-to-government, making peace and winning allies through a series of treaties. The new Constitution in 1789 reserved the regulation of commerce with the tribes to the federal government—specifically in Article I, section 8, clause 3—putting them on the same footing as foreign governments. The First Congress affirmed this principle in major legislation on trade and land deals with Indians—laws that are still in effect. Treaty-making with the United States was the foundation for tribal relations with the new American government. But the legal theory underlying that relationship was sharply contested until Chief Justice John Marshall's pivotal 1832 decision in Cherokee Nation v. Georgia. In declaring tribes to be dependent nations, he started the process by which tribes were recognized under the American federal system, equal in status with state governments as the third leg of sovereign membership, but also diminished in stature under this system.

After declaring independence, the United States signed its first formal treaty with an Indian tribe, the Delaware, at Fort Pitt (now Pittsburgh, Pa.) on September 17, 1778. The mutual defense treaty allowed American troops to pass through the Delaware Tribe's land to attack the British fort at Detroit, Mich. Under the treaty, the United States recognized the Delaware Nation's sovereignty. The treaty also offered significant insight into the later process of incorporating tribes into the federal system. Article VI of the treaty gave the Delaware Nation the option of joining other tribes in the Ohio region to form a state with the Delaware Tribe at the head to become part of the U.S. confederation, with representation in Congress. Although the statehood option was never taken up, it foreshadowed the later acknowledgment of tribes as partners in the federal system."[5]

---

[5] https://www.usmint.gov/coins/coin-medal-programs/native-american-dollar-coins/2013-delaware-treaty-of-1778

2014 Native American Hospitality to the Lewis and Clark Expedition

The reverse design depicts a Native American man offering a pipe while his wife offers provisions of fish, corn, roots and gourds. In the background is a stylized image of the face of William Clark's compass highlighting "NW," the area in which the expedition occurred. The reverse was designed by Chris Costello and sculpted and engraved by Joseph Menna.

"When the Lewis and Clark Expedition crossed the Continental Divide, the nature of its mission fundamentally changed. Up to that point, it had been exploring territory that European powers would recognize as belonging to the United States through the Louisiana Purchase. Once past the headwaters of the Missouri River, the expedition was securing the American claim to a new accession of territory, the Pacific Northwest. More than ever before, success of the mission depended on help from the Indian tribes, who might not have understood the long-term consequences of their hospitality. For every step of their way through the Rocky Mountains to the Pacific Coast, Lewis and Clark depended on the friendship, supplies and logistical support of the tribes on their route. They camped in the midst of the Mandan and Hidatsa tribes in the winter of 1804-05 and the Clatsop in 1806, and their cooperation was essential to the resounding success of this mission.

The Mandan and Hidatsa tribes of the Missouri River welcomed Lewis and Clark and their Corps of Discovery to their unique dome-shaped earthen lodge villages, often sitting and talking by the campfire when meeting with Black Cat, the Mandan chief. The tribes were located in present-day North Dakota. Their village was the central marketplace for the northern plains. Lewis expressed the highest respect for Black Cat (Posecopsahe) and walked miles out of his way to smoke a pipe with him on the day of his departure. The expedition group traded for corn and gathered every scrap of intelligence they could about the route ahead. During the winter at Fort Mandan, the expedition blacksmith forged somewhat eccentric ax heads to trade for corn. Eighteen months later, the expedition found that some of the same ax heads had already been traded to the Nez Perce, which the expedition relied on to supply horses from their famous herd. Down the length of the Columbia River, the Americans traded with the Chinook and other tribes for provisions.

The Clatsop Indians were flourishing people who enjoyed plentiful amounts of fish and fur and occupied three villages on the southern side of the Columbia River. They were located in what is now known as Oregon. Some Clatsop tribesmen complained about the expedition's stinginess with gifts. Coboway, chief of one of the villages, visited the expedition group at its fort, which was still under construction. He exchanged some goods, including a sea otter pelt, for fishhooks and a small bag of Shoshone tobacco. Over the rest of the winter, Coboway would be a frequent and welcome visitor to this area they named Fort Clatsop. The Clatsop also aided the expedition both in preparing for, and dealing with, the northwest winter and informed Lewis and Clark that there was a good amount of elk on the south side of the Columbia, information that influenced the construction of Fort Clatsop where they did. When the expedition's food supplies were running low, the Clatsop informed the corps that a whale had washed ashore some miles to the south.

At the expedition's departure from Fort Clatsop, Lewis wrote in his journal that Coboway "has been much more kind an[d] hospitable to us than any other indian in this neighbourhood." Lewis committed the expedition's one act of pilferage, appropriating a Native canoe for the voyage up the river. (He later encountered a Lumhi Indian who claimed ownership of the vessel and paid him off with an elk skin.) This misdeed remained on the historical record, and late in 2011, the *family of William Clark presented a replica of the original canoe to the Chinook tribe in recompense."*[6]

2015 Mohawk Ironworkers in New York City

The reverse design features a Mohawk ironworker reaching for an I-beam that is swinging into position high above New York City. It honors the Kahnawake Mohawk and Mohawk Akwesasne communities for their "high iron" construction work and the building of skyscrapers in New York City. The reverse was designed and sculpted by Ronald D. Sanders and engraved by Phebe Hemphill.

"In the coin's image, a Mohawk ironworker reaches for an I-beam that is swinging into position high above the city. Two rivets decorate the border, one on each side, and "Mohawk Ironworkers" is inscribed at the bottom. The required inscriptions "United States of America" and "$1" are also present.

Native American tribes take great pride in the bravery of their people, whether displayed in high-iron construction work or fire jumping and brake cutting to handle the West's raging wildfires. As warriors were honored in days past, these workers are honored for putting their lives on the line to protect the people's safety and welfare.

The tradition of Mohawk high iron working dates to 1886. Mohawk day laborers on a local bridge project insisted on working on the bridge itself. The supervisors were amazed at the Mohawk's ability to handle heights.

But the work was dangerous, and the danger became clear in 1907. The Quebec Bridge, designed to be the largest cantilevered bridge in

[6] https://www.usmint.gov/coins/coin-medal-programs/native-american-dollar-coins/2014-native-american-hospitality-to-lewis-clark-expedition

the world, collapsed, killing 33 Mohawk workers. Four family names were wiped out. After the disaster, the Kahnawake Clan Mothers ruled that large numbers of Mohawk men could not work on the same project at the same time.

As the 20th century progressed and the number of huge iron structures increased, the demand for these ironworkers increased as well. New York City in particular was reaching for the skies using crews from the Kahnawake and the Mohawk Akwesasne communities from upstate New York and Canada. At one point, one in four Akwesasne men worked in high-rise construction.

When the World Trade Center was attacked on September 11, 2001, a Mohawk construction crew saw it up close from a nearby building. When debris needed to be removed, dozens of Mohawk ironworkers volunteered for the dangerous job. It was thanks to a Mohawk worker from Akwesasne that the "9-11" flag was displayed at the 2004 Winter Olympics. He recovered the flag from Six World Trade Center's lobby on the day after the attack. Just as the ancient Native American warriors devoted themselves to preserving all the people of the tribe, the modern risk-takers see their occupations as a contribution to the public good. These contributions have inspired the design of this coin." [7]

---

[7] https://www.usmint.gov/learn/kids/coins-and-medals/native-american-dollar-coins/2015-coin-mohawk-ironworkers

2016 Code Talkers

The reverse design features two helmets—one in the shape of the U.S. helmets used in World War I and the other in the shape of a World War II helmet. Behind the helmets are two feathers that form a "V," symbolizing victory, unity and the important role that the code talkers played in both world wars. The reverse was designed by Thomas D. Rogers and sculpted and engraved by Renata Gordon.

"It is estimated that more than 12,000 Native Americans served in the U.S. military during World War I. In World War II, more than 44,000 Native Americans, out of a total Native American population of less than 350,000, served with distinction in both the European and Pacific theaters. Hundreds played a vital communications role in both world wars. This select group of Native Americans was asked to develop and use secret battle codes using their native languages to communicate troop movements and enemy positions. Their efforts saved many lives because America's enemies were unable to decode their messages.

Native languages came to play an increasingly vital role in the U.S. war effort in both World War I and II. Several tribes provided Native American speakers for telephone squads on the French battlefields in World War I. Additional tribes sent soldiers to join the code talkers of World War II, serving in North Africa, Italy, France and the Pacific. The languages used by American Indians greatly assisted their fellow American soldiers in the heat of battle by transmitting messages in unbreakable battle codes. The Navajo code talkers from the World War II Pacific Theater were the most famous group, numbering approximately 420 by the end of the war."[8]

---

[8] https://www.usmint.gov/coins/coin-medal-programs/native-american-dollar-coins/2016-native-american-code-talkers

2017 Sequoyah

The reverse design features a profile of Sequoyah writing "Sequoyah from Cherokee Nation" in syllabary along the border of the design. The reverse was designed by Chris Costello and was sculpted by Charles L. Vickers.

"Sequoyah adapted writing to the Cherokee language by devising symbols for each syllable. His achievement is one of a handful of examples in world history regarding the development of an original writing system. After 12 years of work, Sequoyah unveiled the alphabet in a demonstration with his daughter Ah-yo-ka. News spread quickly and Cherokees flocked to learn the system. In 1821, the Cherokee Nation adopted it as its own. Within months, thousands of Cherokee became literate.

The Cherokee Syllabary gave birth to Native American journalism. The first American Indian newspaper, the Cherokee Phoenix, included editorials which embodied the Cherokees' determination to retain their lands, news on activities of the Cherokee government, as well as relations with the federal and state governments. This written language helped create a dialogue between Cherokee Nation and the United States Government, and assisted in the preservation of interests, hopes and struggles of individuals during a unique time in our history."[9]

---

[9] https://www.usmint.gov/coins/coin-medal-programs/native-american-dollar-coins/2017-sequoyah

2018 Jim Thorpe

The reverse design depicts Jim Thorpe, while the foreground highlights his achievements in football and as an Olympian. The reverse was sculpted and engraved by Michael Gaudioso.

"James Francis "Jim" Thorpe (1888-1953), was born near Prague, Oklahoma, in what was then Indian Territory. Raised in the Sac and Fox tribe, he was given the native name Wa-Tho-Huk, meaning "Bright Path." Jim Thorpe became possibly the most versatile natural athlete of the early 20th century. After a difficult youth, running away from school after several family crises, Thorpe came into his own at the Carlisle Indian Industrial School in Carlisle, Pennsylvania. Although the residential Indian school had a mixed reputation, Carlisle then had the services of one of the great early football coaches, Glenn Scobey "Pop" Warner and it fielded a national championship football team, led by Thorpe. At the time Thorpe was the core of the school's track and field team, also coached by Warner, and the story is that Warner was reluctant to let his track star run the risk of playing football.

Thorpe was named to the All-American first team in 1911 and 1912. In 1911, Carlisle upset Harvard 18-15, as Thorpe scored all its points, four field goals and a touchdown. In 1912, Carlisle won the national collegiate championship. It beat Army 27-6; a cadet named Dwight D. Eisenhower injured his knee trying to tackle Thorpe.

In 1912, Thorpe represented the U. S. at the Summer Olympics in Stockholm, Sweden, competing in the new Pentathlon and Decathlon as well as two field events. He easily won both multi-event medals, finishing first in eight of the combined 15 events. His point record stood for two decades. In an often-told story, King Gustav V of Sweden, presenting Thorpe a special decathlon award, told him, "You are the greatest athlete in the world," and Thorpe replied, "Thanks, king."

Thorpe then embarked on an incredibly varied career with the public flocking to his professional appearances in football, baseball and basketball. He played for six teams in what later became the National Football League. In 1922, he became the first president of the American Professional Football Association, precursor of the NFL. In baseball, he played for the New York Giants, the Cincinnati Reds and the Boston Braves. He also organized an all-Indian football team, reuniting some Carlisle players. Today, sports writers rank him at the top of their lists of greatest athletes of the 20th Century."[10]

More to Come?

The Native American $1 Coin Program does not specify how many distinctive reverse designs will be produced. The design for each reverse is determined by the Secretary of the Treasury in consultation with the U.S. Senate Committee on Indian Affairs, the Congressional Native American Caucus of the U.S. House of Representatives, the Commission of Fine Arts and the National Congress of American Indians, and undergoes a public review by the Citizens Coinage Advisory Committee. There are many more Native American individuals and events that merit consideration for commemoration in this series, so hopefully there will be many more distinctive reverse designs before this series comes to an end.

---

[10] https://www.usmint.gov/coins/coin-medal-programs/native-american-dollar-coins/2018-jim-thorpe

REFERENCES

Bowers, Q. David. (2007). *A Guide Book of Buffalo and Jefferson Nickels*. Racine, WI: Whitman Publishing.

https://coins.thefuntimesguide.com/american-indian-coin/

http://earlycommemorativecoins.com/1934-1938-daniel-boone-bicentennial-half-dollar/

https://en.wikipedia.org/wiki/Blackfish_(Shawnee_leader)

https://www.usmint.gov

Kuhl, Jason F. (2001). "The portrayal of native Americans on U.S. Coinage." *The Numismatist* 114(2), February, 150-155.

McCreight, Major. (1943). *The Wigwam: Puffs from the Peace Pipe*. Sykesville, PA: Nupp Printing Co.

"New Idea in Gold Coins: The 1908 Pieces Have Figure below the Surface Instead of in Relief." (1908). *The New York Times*, November 12.

Pike, William E. (1999). "James Earle Fraser: Legacy of the West." *The Numismatist* 112(11), November, 1292-1295.

Pine Ridge Reservation Web Site (Accessed 7 May 2014). http://www.home.comcast.net/~zebrec/Chief_Iron_Tail.htm.

Sprague, Donovin A. (2004). Charleston, SC: Arcadia Publishing.

Taxay, D. (ed.) (1971). *Scott's Comprehensive Catalogue and Encyclopedia of U.S. Coins*. New York: Scott Publishing Co.

U. S. Mint Web Site. Accessed 7 May 2014. http://www.usmint.gov/mint_programs/golden_dollar_coin.

Yoeman, R.S. (2000). *A Guide Book of United States Coins*. New York: St. Martin's Press.

ABOUT THE AUTHOR

Vic Sower began studying and collecting coins when he was 10 years old and was a long-time member of the American Numismatic Association. He has degrees in chemistry and operations management. His career is about equally split between working in industry and teaching in a university. His currently is an author and quality management consultant and is Distinguished Professor Emeritus at Sam Houston State University. He is married and is the father of two children and the grandfather of five grandchildren.